Sans Souci

Gert Streidt
Roland Handrick

Sans Souci

Potsdam Palaces
and Gardens

RV Verlag

© RV Reise- und Verkehrsverlag GmbH,
Berlin · Gütersloh · Leipzig · Munich · Potsdam · Stuttgart 1993

Author: Gert Streidt, Potsdam-Sans Souci Palaces and Gardens
Foundation
Cover illustration: Sans Souci Palace with the vineyard, Roland
Handrick, Potsdam-Sans Souci Palaces and Gardens Foundation
Map/Cartography on the last cover page: RV Reise- und
Verkehrsverlag GmbH, Berlin · Gütersloh · Leipzig · Munich
Potsdam · Stuttgart
Plans of the tours: Vivien Taschner, Potsdam

Illustrations: Gert Streidt, Potsdam, pages 6/7, Potsdam-Sans
Souci Palaces and Gardens Foundation, pages 64, 86
All other pictures by Roland Handrick, Potsdam

Conception, administration, coordination: Beatrice Weber,
Prisma Verlag GmbH, Munich
Layout/typesetting: Bärbel Jehle, Prisma Verlag GmbH, Munich
Translation: Anthony Crawford, ÜMS Berlin
Reproduction: Liton, Mailand, printex, Verona
Cover design: Prisma Verlag GmbH, Munich
Printed by Mohndruck Graphische Betriebe, Gütersloh

Printed in Germany
ISBN 3−575−11081−6

Table of Contents

Sans Souci Palace with the Vineyard, the Picture Gallery (right), the New Chambers (left) and the Mount of Ruins (background).

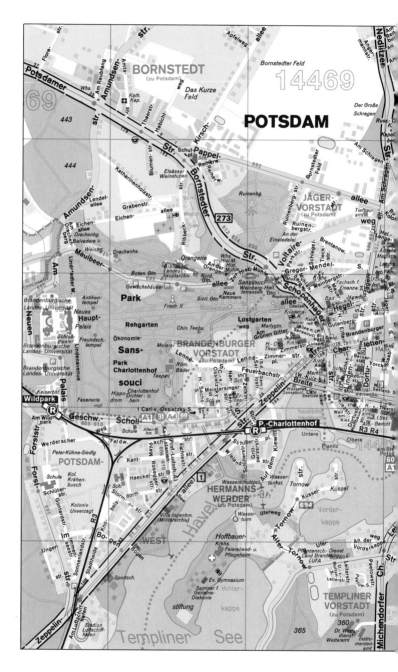

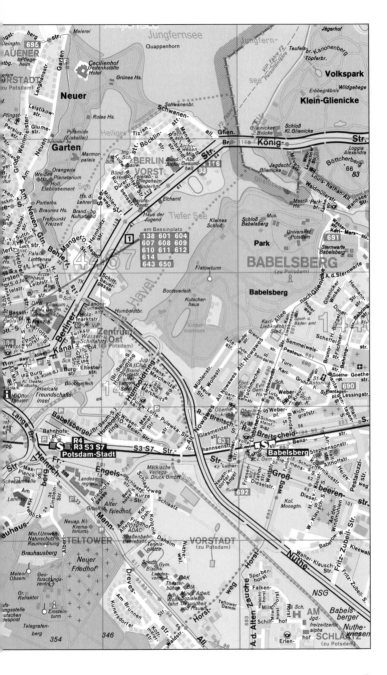

The Great Elector with his consort Louisa Henrietta.
Portrait by Pieter Nason.
Page 2: Air. Marble, by Lambert Sigisbert Adam.

10

About the Origins
of the Potsdam Garden Landscape

»The whole island must be made a Paradise...«

 Potsdam would have remained a small, insignificant country marketplace if the Great Elector (1620–1688) had not taken a liking to the town and, after the Thirty Years' War, begun to build a town palace there. The Elector's artistic conceptions were decisively influenced by his governor at Cleves, the well-travelled Johann Moritz von Nassau-Siegen (1604–1679), who advised his Majesty in a letter of 1664 to transform »the whole island« into »a Paradise«. Consequently, a wreath of pleasure palaces, connected to one another by avenues, was built round about Potsdam – the palace in Caputh has been preserved until today. In deciding to establish a second seat for his court outside Berlin at Potsdam, the Great Elector initiated a building tradition upheld by all his successors.

Potsdam thus became an electoral residence and, until the abdication of the last emperor in 1918, the cultural standard and the artistic orientation of the House of Hohenzollern played a decisive role in the development of the city. The landscaping efforts of the Great Elector have already been mentioned above. Frederick I (1657–1713), who in 1701 became the first Hohenzollern to wear the royal crown of Prussia, commissioned architects to build the majestic buildings he needed to represent his new status. Frederick William I (1688–1740), the Soldier King, ordered the construction of simple townhouses along the street now called *Gutenbergstrasse,* as well as the building of a mathematically subdivided street system.

The latter monarch took Holland, then in an advanced stage of development, as his example and brought Dutch craftsmen into the country, building a »Dutch Quarter« for them. This quarter is preserved today, as is the hunting lodge erected in similar fashion at the »Stern«. On this former extensive hunting ground, modern blocks have only recently been built, but the name of the district has not changed. Frederick William I also ordered the construction of the famous Garrison Church. Topped with an 80-metre-high

11

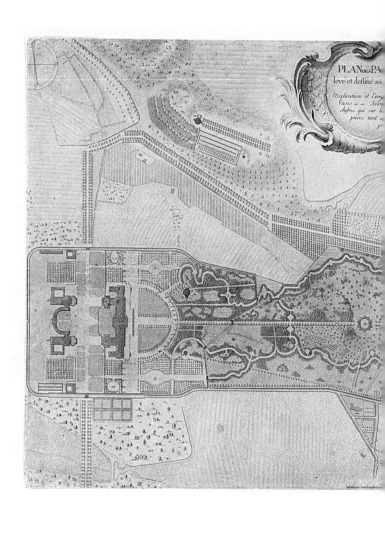

Sans Souci Park. Plan by Friedrich Zacharias Saltzmann, 1772.

12

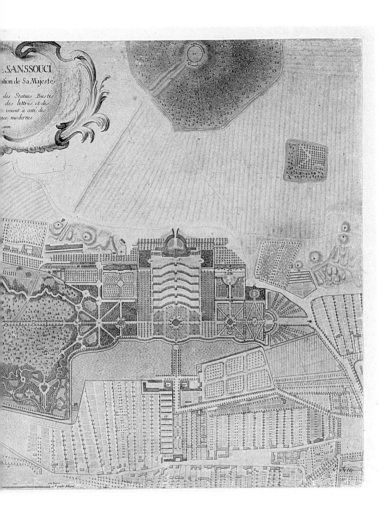

SANSSOUCI
tion de Sa Majesté

des Statues Bustes
des lettres et des
voient à coté des
ne modernes

Hall in Stern Hunting Lodge.

steeple, this building characterized Potsdam's skyline until its demolition in the sixties (the church had been heavily damaged in World War II).

The town was developed considerably under Frederick the Great (1712–1786). This sovereign employed many prominent artists, including the architect Georg Wenzeslaus von Knobelsdorff, the sculptor Friedrich Christian Glume and the French painter Antoine Pesne, and fostered an artistic style known in art history as Friderician Rococo. The king was tireless in his concern for the architectural ornamentation of the town. Gradually, a grandiose ensemble arose whose artificiality must have not only fascinated, but also astonished the observer. In 1744, Frederick had a vineyard planted outside the town gates, on the so-called Desert Hill. Thus began the history of Sans Souci.

Even in the 18th century, the park with the vineyard palace and other buildings gained fame far beyond the borders of Prussia. Built upon a natural hill, the palace is fitted into the surrounding landscape. The view from the uppermost terrace of the vineyard reached far over the Havel lake country. Laying out this park was

Equestrian statue of Frederick the Great. Copy after C. D. Rauch.

the first step in the realization of a great project: the shaping of the Potsdam landscape, an enterprise concluded in the 19th century by Peter Joseph Lenné.

Frederick the Great's successor, Frederick William II (1741–1797), sought to distance himself from his great ancestor. He chose a location outside the town, on the banks of the *Heiliger See*, to lay out a »New Garden« and to build another palace. This construction, the Marble Palace, exudes an atmosphere rather of civility than of royal ostentation. The palace and its park were originally more like a peaceful island removed from reality. But after 1817, Lenné altered the place: by means of composed vistas, he integrated palace and park into the surrounding landscape.

If Frederick William III (1770–1840) was little active in Potsdam, his two eldest sons, the princes Frederick William (later King Frederick William IV, 1795–1861) and William (later Emperor William I, 1797–1888), were all the more so. In the service of these two rulers, the architect Karl Friedrich Schinkel and the landscape gardener Peter Joseph Lenné created a man-made landscape of truly European magnitude. During this period, the Charlotten-

Peter Joseph Lenné. Lithograph after Franz Krüger.

hof and Babelsberg Parks were laid out (the former as an extension of Sans Souci Park), and the palaces of the same names were built. Frederick William IV, an artistically gifted king who initiated many projects and constantly furnished new ideas, commis sioned Lenné to realize a great project. In the endeavour to »unite harmoniously, through an embellished landscape, all the historical beauties scattered over the environs of Potsdam«, Lenné integrated the entire countryside surrounding the city in a grandiose, unifying composition.

The German Empire left Potsdam with great, majestic public buildings which even today substantially determine the city's appearance. After Germany had been united and the German Empire founded, it was mainly Emperor William II (1859 to 1941) who sought to express his country's new status as a great power by having plans drawn for colossal buildings. The Emperor chose the New Palace as his residence during his sojourns in Potsdam and had his own railway station, the *Kaiserbahnhof*, built nearby.

When the last Hohenzollern emperor abdicated in 1918, the palaces and gardens in Potsdam became state-owned museums. Since then, generations of museologists working in Sans Souci have endeavoured to preserve and care for the precious heritage entrusted to them.

The historic centre of Potsdam was destroyed in the terrific bombardment of April 14th, 1945, but the palaces and gardens were largely spared from destruction during World War II. After the war, the city centre was rebuilt with disregard for the original plan. Thus the visitor will never be able to relive the beauty of old Potsdam. The opportunities resulting from the opening of the Berlin Wall in November of 1989 are all the more important, though, for now the garden landscape in and around Potsdam, created by Lenné in the 19th century and in large part preserved until today, can once again be visited and experienced as a whole.

With the inclusion of the Potsdam man-made landscape in the UNESCO World Heritage List in 1990, the international community paid homage to this ensemble combining architecture and landscape gardens. The present publication is devoted to the heart of this ensemble: Sans Souci Park, the New Garden and Babelsberg Park. It is intended as a companion for the visitor interested in getting to know the beauties of these gardens.

The tours described in the following pages are conceived so that the visitor can always appreciate the individual features in their context, and find inspiration for further walks in this wonderful park landscape.

17

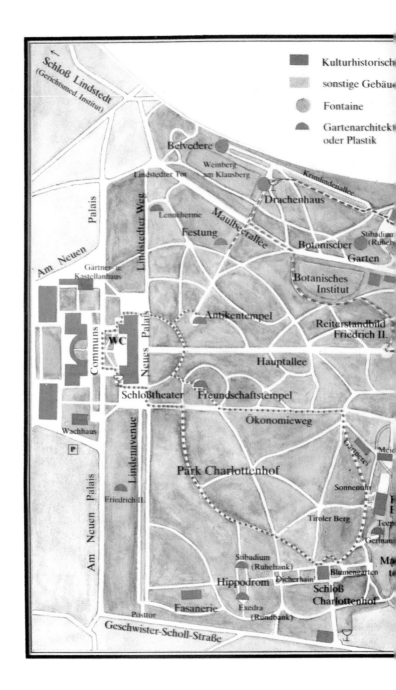

Schloß Lindstedt
(Gerichtsmed. Institut)

Kulturhistorisch

sonstige Gebäu

Fontaine

Gartenarchitekt
oder Plastik

Belvedere

Weinberg
am Klausberg

Lindstedter Tor

Krimlindenallee

Drachenhaus

Lindstedter Weg

Palais

Am Neuen

Lenneherme

Festung

Maulbeerallee

Botanischer

Stibadium
(Ruheb

Garten

Gärtner- u.
Kastellanhaus

Botanisches
Institut

Communs

Neues Palais

Antikentempel

WC

Reiterstandbild
Friedrich II.

Hauptallee

Schloßtheater

Freundschaftstempel

Wachhaus

Okonomieweg

P

Lindenavenue

Park Charlottenhof

Sonnenuhr

Meie

Friedrich II.

Am Neuen Palais

Tiroler Berg

Teep

German

Stibadium
(Ruhebank)

Dichterhain

Blumengarten

Hippodrom

Fasanerie

Exedra
(Rundbank)

Schloß
Charlottenhof

Posttor

Geschwister-Scholl-Straße

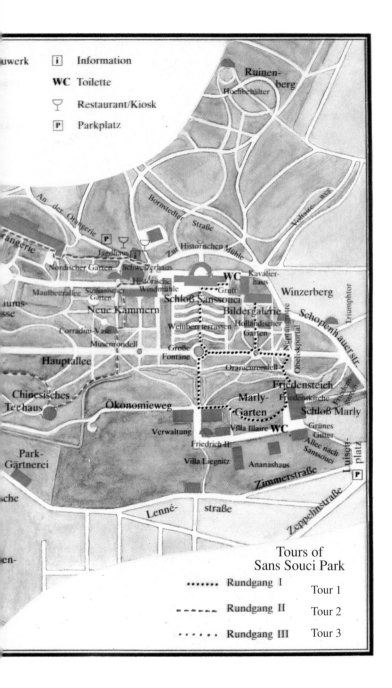

The Pump House in the shape of a mosque.

Sans Souci Park: Tour 1
From Sans Souci Palace to the
Church of Peace

**Sans Souci Palace • Vineyard • Great Fontain Circle
Picture Gallery • Neptune Grotto • Obelisk Portal
Church of Peace • Emperor Frederick Mausoleum
Marly Garden • Sans Souci Palace**

The tour begins in the forecourt of **Sans Souci Palace**. The court is enclosed by a double colonnade of paired Corinthian columns. Where these meet the palace, the Corinthian motif carries over to the façade, the columns becoming pilasters (rectangular projecting columns). The front of the palace is offered to the visitor's view: this »official« side, directly accessible from the town, is hardly majestic but rather modestly styled. The visitor looks in vain for a clue to the former proprietors and occupants: there is no coat of arms, no statue here. Frederick the Great (1712–1786), King of Prussia, wanted to be left in peace in his summer residence. The name of Sans Souci (in English: carefree) tells of the king's desire: for Frederick the Great, this was not a place for royal ostentation – the great town palaces of Berlin and Potsdam already had this function. Sans Souci was rather a private, intimate hermitage, a place of personal retreat. This is also apparent in the decoration of the interior.

Through the central opening in the colonnade, the visitor can see the Mount of Ruins. The buildings on this hill were originally erected as ruins at Frederick the Great's orders. This was in keeping with the taste of the 18th century: many princes had their gardens ornamented with artificial ruins, which were to remind one of the transience of this life. The ruins were usually patterned after classical antiquity, for the rediscovery of the beauty of ancient architecture had begun in the mid-18th century, fostered by the writings of Johann Joachim Winckelmann. The Mount of Ruins too borrows from antiquity: a wall that reminds one of the Colosseum in Rome, a dilapidated temple and a pyramid. The tower was first added a hundred years after the other ruins had been built. The buildings surround a large pool that was meant to supply the fountains in the park. Although Frederick the Great invested an immense amount of money in the project, it failed repeatedly due to techni-

cal difficulties. It proved impossible to pump enough water from the Havel River up to the Mount of Ruins to operate the fountains. Only once, on a spring day in 1754, did Frederick see a fountain in Sans Souci: the gardeners had collected enough snow in the pool during the winter to present the king with a feeble, splashing fountain.

The fountain plans had to wait almost a century before King Frederick William IV (1795–1861) took them up again and realized them with the help of steam power. He had a pump house built in the shape of a mosque on the Neustadt Bay of the Havel, in what is now the *Breite Strasse*, from whence water was pumped up to the pool on the Mount of Ruins. The same strategy is still in use today, except that the pumps are now driven by modern electric motors. The original steam engine from the year 1843 is still preserved, however, and visitors to the pump house can see it in operation.

To return to Sans Souci: the palace was built between 1745 and 1747 from designs by Georg Wenzeslaus von Knobelsdorff (1699–1753). Until his early death, this artist was Frederick the Great's favorite architect, and art historians also name Knobelsdorff among the outstanding German architects of the first half of the 18th century. His ideas regarding architecture are characterized by a convincing combination of late baroque and rococo elements

Sans Souci Park. Plan by Gustav Meyer, 1853.

22

The Mount of Ruins.

with those of early Classicism. Ancient architecture, which Knobelsdorff studied during travels in Italy, and modern French architecture, which he experienced during a stay in France, were determining influences for this artist. Knobelsdorff's architecture is well-proportioned and of a reserved, discreet lightness and elegance.

In building the palace, Knobelsdorff cleverly managed to bow to his royal patron's wishes without having to sacrifice his own ideas. In those years, Frederick the Great's artistic conceptions closely followed the Rococo, the French taste current in the mid-18th century. The name of this style is derived from the term »rocaille,« referring to ornamental shellwork. The basic form of rococo ornamentation, the *rocaille*, is a shell curled into a C-shaped scroll. Rococo is above all an interior style. In the quest for intimacy and comfort, the room decorations were subordinate to a comprehensive design concept. Ornamentation unite all room elements, and make them form a harmonious whole. The rooms in Sans Souci Palace rank among the finest achievements of German rococo interior design.

The tour of the palace begins in the Vestibule (entrance hall). The Corinthian motif encountered in the façade and the double colonnade appears here as well. Pairs of columns structure the room and give it a cool elegance. Only the painted ceiling offers a

23

hint of the cheerfulness typical of Rococo: the goddess Flora greets us with flowers and fruits. The vineyard theme is taken up by the ornamentation of the doors, as well as by the reliefs above, which depict scenes from the myth of Bacchus, the god of wine.

Through a side door, the visitor passes from the Vestibule into the Small Gallery. This is a long, narrow room in which Frederick kept a part of his art collection. Niches in the wall opposite the windows hold ancient sculptures (Bacchus, Athena, Apollo and Pan, the god of shepherds). Paintings adorn the wall between the niches. Until World War II, a collection of works by the French painter Antoine Watteau (1684–1721) was found here. Frederick held this artist in extraordinarily high esteem, most likely because he recognized many of his own feelings as well as his own philosophy of life in Watteau's softly melancholic scenes. The paintings were removed during the war but have not yet been returned to Sans Souci. Today, the visitor can see here mainly works by two of Watteau's disciples: Jean Baptiste Pater (1696–1726) and Nicolas Lancret (1690–1743). Both artists stayed true to their master's tradition.

In this room too, the gilded vine garlands decorating the mirrors remind us that we are in a vineyard palace. A bust of Frederick the Great is found on the mantelpiece at the end of the Gallery. This sculpture is a fairly authentic image of the king, for it was modelled after his death mask by the sculptor Johann Eckstein. Frederick the Great died at Sans Souci on August 17th, 1786, at the age of 74.

The Library is not only the most personal room in the palace, but also the most impressive from the standpoint of art history. Separated from the other rooms, it is only accessible through a narrow corridor. Balanced proportions and warm colours lend this room an atmosphere of harmony and calm. The cedar wall panelling is decorated with gilded bronze ornaments. A mood conducive to reflection and mental concentration reigns in the Library. The visitor may appreciate the design of the interior only through a window in the door, for guided tours of nearly 40 people would cause a sudden rise in humidity and pose substantial restoration problems. Like the rest of the living quarters, the Library is situated on the garden side of the palace, facing the south.

The visitor enters next the Study and Bedchamber. The death chair of Frederick the Great is displayed in the alcove. In 1786, the year of the king's death, the room was remodelled in the classic style. The decor appears sober and practical, almost cool. But in the adjoining room, the Concert Chamber, the diversity of forms, characteristic of Rococo, surprises the visitor again. The imaginative,

24

G. W. von Knobelsdorff. Copy of a portrait by A. Pesne.

Sans Souci Palace, Library.

playful and vital ornamentation unites this interior to a single work of art. Nowhere does the eye come to rest – the unifying momentum of the *rocaille* scrolls constantly invites the visitor to look and wonder further. The mirrors opposite the windows enlarge the room and connect it with the garden. In the lateral mirrors, the ornamentation is multiplied, which makes the room appear even richer. It seems almost as though a musical composition by Carl Philipp Emanuel Bach (1714–1788) or Frederick the Great were embodied in the rhythm of the ornamentation.

Sans Souci Palace, Marble Hall.

Music rooms are found in all the dwellings furnished for Frederick. The Prussian king was a man exceptionally favoured by the Muses: he was an enthusiastic art collector, wrote poetry and concerned himself with architecture. But his special passion was music. He played the flute (a reproduction of his instrument is displayed on the piano) and was the composer of four symphonies and over 120 flute sonatas. In his chamber orchestra, Frederick engaged such excellent musicians as Carl Philipp Emanuel Bach and Franz Benda (1709–1786).

The large murals in the Concert Chamber are illustrations of scenes from the *Metamorphoses*, a compilation of poems by the Roman Ovid. The paintings are by Antoine Pesne (1683–1757), Frederick's court painter. These bright and vital murals are perfectly suited to the wall decoration.

In the next room, the Reception Room, Pesne created the painting on the ceiling. As before in the Vestibule, Flora appears in the centre of this picture. Here she is portrayed accompanied by her lover Zephyr, the god of the mild west wind. In fact, the royal apartments begin with the Reception Room but for practical reasons, they are visited in reverse order.

The Marble Hall, crowned by a cupola, occupies the centre of the palace. Like the forecourt and the Vestibule, this room is structured by Corinthian columns, here executed as monoliths of precious Carrara marble. Tall French windows open on the vineyard and the connection between palace and garden is suggested by the coloured inlays of the marble floor, featuring various stylized plants. Since the Marble Hall stays cool while the terrace is sun-drenched, the king used to withdraw to this room for refreshment. Here, Frederick the Great offered his guests legendary banquets; here he met with intellectuals from all over the world in philosophical discussions. The most prominent participant at these mee-

Sans Souci Palace, Concert Chamber.

View of the garden.

tings was the Frenchman Voltaire, whose years of friendship with the king were intense and often stormy.

The west wing of the palace is devoted to Guest Rooms. Originally these were to be the queen's apartments, but Frederick's consort, Elizabeth Christine, never lived in Sans Souci. She usually resided at the Niederschönhausen Palace or at the town palace in Berlin. The doors of the Guest Rooms, like those of the royal apartments, are positioned in enfilade, i.e. along a single axis. The rooms are also decorated in rococo style, although less lavishly than the king's apartments. Each Guest Room has an adjoining servant's chamber. The exit to the forecourt is reached by passing through these chambers.

A visit to the Ladies' Wing of the palace (entrance on the west side) is recommended for those who have time. This wing was built under King Frederick William IV, who had apartments in Sans Souci furnished in 1840. The Ladies' Wing accommodates guest rooms which are considered an interesting specimen of courtly living in the mid-19th century.

Leaving the forecourt, the visitor goes around the palace and comes to the garden side. In contrast to the modestly designed north façade, that on the garden side is enlivened by 36 bacchants carved in sandstone. These sculptures rank among the most beautiful works of Christian Glume (1714–1752), an artist who did a

Sans Souci Palace, garden side.

great deal of work for Frederick. The sculptures depicting wine worshippers mediate between the vineyard and the palace, whose interior decoration is dominated by variations on the vineyard theme.

The tomb of Frederick the Great, bordered by busts of Roman emperors arranged in a semicircle, is to be found at the eastern end of the broad palace terrace. As early as 1744, at the age of 32, Frederick had decided that he wanted to be buried at Sans Souci. Near the tomb is a marble statue by the French sculptor François Gaspard Adam (1710–1761), representing Flora and Zephyr. These two divinities from classical mythology have already been encountered in the painting on the ceiling of the Reception Room in Sans Souci Palace.

The 132 steps of the great stairway lead down the vineyard hillside to the parterre. But before descending, the visitor should take a moment to enjoy the panoramic view from the uppermost terrace. To the left in the distance, in the centre of Potsdam, appears the cupola of St. Nicholas' Church, built by Schinkel.

Thanks to extensive restoration works done between 1979 and 1983, the **vineyard** has now regained the appearance it had in

Tomb of Frederick the Great.

1744. The current vegetation is also in keeping with the original: fig trees grow in glass-covered niches in the retaining walls, while grapevines climb the trellises between the niches. Now that restoration is complete, palace and vineyard are again in harmony with one another, and the visitor looking from the **Great Fountain Circle** up to the vineyard can savour a world-famous view. In the art history, there are but few examples of vineyards associated with palatial architecture. In Sans Souci, this association is due to Frederick the Great's deep-seated sympathy for gardening. The king expressly wished that decorative and useful gardening be combined at his summer residence. Here, in the heart of the park, it is still possible (in spite of many transformations) to recognize various elements of the baroque garden: geometric lawns, flower beds, trimmed hedges and trees, straight ditches, a fountain basin and finally, a great number of bright white marble sculptures, forming a stimulating contrast to the green of the flora. The twelve sculptures surrounding the Great Fountain represent the four Elements (Water, Fire, Earth, Air) and the Olympian gods Venus, Mercury, Apollo, Diana, Juno, Jupiter, Mars and Minerva. That air pollutants and natural weathering have left their marks on the statues

31

cannot be overlooked. The restorers of Sans Souci are doing all that is within their power to combat the deterioration. Many of the nearly 400 marble sculptures in the park must undergo preservative treatment, but others can only be stored away and replaced with reproductions.

Semicircular benches placed between the statues in the Great Fountain Circle invite the visitor to pause. The benches were added in the 19th century, as were the tall columns, crowned with copies of ancient sculptures, which decorate the lawns. The main avenue leads in a straight line east and west from here, dividing the entire park along a length of about 2.5 km. From the circles formed by widenings in the avenue, the visitor can enjoy ever new and surprising views of the different gardens with their buildings and sculptures.

The tour carries on eastward, in the direction of the obelisk. To the left and right, fountain walls with marble baths mark the border of the part of the garden directly related to Sans Souci Palace. The baths are purely decorative and have never been used for bathing.

The visitor comes now to a part of the garden characterized by hedged plots in geometrical shapes. In the 18th century, fruit and vegetables were grown in these plots. A small fountain circle

Interior of the Picture Gallery.

32

Picture Gallery.

marks the centre of the garden and eight paths radiate from here. The pedestals originally supported marble busts of members of the House of Orange, a line of Dutch princes related to the Hohenzollern. This is why the area is called the Dutch Garden. However, the busts were severely weather-damaged and had to be stored away.

The remarkably broad north-south axis, which crosses the main avenue here, offers a view of the most outstanding building in the Dutch Garden: the **Picture Gallery**. Like Sans Souci Palace, this is a wide-set, single-storey building, accented in the middle by a cupola. Designed by the architect Johann Gottfried Büring (1723–1766) and built from 1755 to 1764, the Picture Gallery reflects Frederick the Great's passion for art collecting. By ordering the construction of a special gallery building for his extensive collection of paintings, Frederick the Great originated one of the first museum buildings in Germany.

The sculptures placed against the façade between the large windows form a transition from the building to the garden. These allegorical figures are worth a closer look, for they represent themes related to the function of the building: Philosophy, History, Sculpture, Painting, Geography, Optics, Astronomy, and Drawing (west

33

Obelisk Portal.

wing, from left to right); Architecture and Truth Found in Nature (central projection); the Imitation of Nature, the Artist's Humours, the Study of the Ancients, Harmony, Engraving, Geometry, and the Cultivation of Art (east wing). The sculptures are by the Germans Johann Gottlieb Heymüller (1715–1763) and Johann Peter Benckert (1709–1765), and the Italians Giuseppe Girola and Felice Cocci. The keystones of the windows arches are decorated with sculpted portraits of famous artists.

The gallery's interior consists of a single hall, whose exquisite, harmoniously matched decorations form a festive background for the paintings displayed here. The pictures hang on the wall opposite the windows, closely arranged side by side and one above another. Here the emphasis is rather on the total effect of the room than on the individual artworks. Nonetheless, masterpieces such as Caravaggio's *Doubting Thomas*, as well as several works by Peter Paul Rubens, are found among the 124 paintings by Italian, French and Flemish artists displayed in this gallery.

For the purpose of restoration, the Picture Gallery will remain closed from 1993 to 1995. The marble tiles of the floor will be renewed and the ornamentation partially re-gilt. In order to improve the conservation of the pictures, a heating system will be installed.

Neptune Grotto.

Detrimental factors such as extreme variations of temperature or excessive humidity can then be eliminated.

The Picture Gallery will thus be a model for the other palaces in Sans Souci Park which will, in their turn, have heating installed. Only in this way can the conservation of the buildings and the works of art they shelter be lastingly assured.

From the sunny terrace below the Picture Gallery, the visitor is offered a view of the Dutch Garden with its masterfully cut yew trees and its amusing Cherubs' Wall. The tour continues eastward along the main avenue. Soon, the visitor comes to the small Moorish Circle. Two of the Moorish busts that once stood here are now exhibited in the Small Gallery in Sans Souci Palace. A small building, the **Neptune Grotto** (1751–1757, by Knobelsdorff) sets an architectural accent in this part of the garden. Furthermore, the grotto was intended as part of the fountain system planned by Frederick the Great.

The **Obelisk Portal** (1747, by Knobelsdorff) is but a few steps from here. This edifice was originally designed as the exit from the garden. But today, many visitors arriving from the city enter the park here through the small gate set in a low iron grille framed between groups of four Corinthian columns. The ornamentation of

View of the Peace Pond and the east side of the Church of Peace.

the portal, sculpted by Friedrich Christian Glume, uses the gardening theme. Flora, goddess of flowers, and Pomona, goddess of fruit trees, stand on the balustrade on either side of the portal, symbolizing the combination of decorative and useful gardening found at Sans Souci. On the portal's central axis rises the Obelisk (1748, by Knobelsdorff). This stone pillar marks the beginning of the main avenue, at whose far western end the radiant New Palace can be seen.

To the right of the Obelisk Portal, the visitor sees the **Church of Peace**, whose nave extends into an artificial pond. This architectural ensemble was created a hundred years after Sans Souci Palace. The visitor walks from the Moorish Circle down an arboured path, then through the »Christ Gate« and the hypostyle hall along the waterside, and finally comes to the Church of Peace.

Commissioned by Frederick William IV, this church was built between 1844 and 1854 after designs by Schinkel's disciple Ludwig Persius (1803–1845). In building a »Church of Peace« during the agitated years of his reign, Frederick William IV wanted to suggest a social renewal in the spirit of early Christian communities. The church design attempts to express this ideal. Italian models, including the Church of San Clemente in Rome, are evident. Like an early Christian basilica, the Church of Peace has a three-bayed nave, and the conscious reference to early Christian art can also be found in the interior, which is decorated in precious materials. Beneath the church is the crypt where Frederick William IV and his consort Elizabeth (1801–1873) are buried.

A second Hohenzollern ruler was also laid to eternal rest here: in front of the church, the **Emperor Frederick Mausoleum** was added onto the atrium by Julius Raschdorf (1823–1914) as a tomb for Emperor Frederick III (1831–1888) and his consort Victoria (1840–1901). The mausoleum is a reproduction of the burial chapel at Innichen in the southern Tirol.

Two garden plots belong to the Church of Peace, both of which were created by Peter Joseph Lenné. Eastward, toward the city, lies the Peace Garden with the pond of the same name. And the **Marly Garden**, a small, intimate landscape garden, extends to the west of the church.

A gently modelled lawn, surrounded by dense vegetation, forms the centre of the Marly Garden, which also contains a remarkable assortment of trees. Walking on the path that circles the central lawn, the visitor can admire ever-changing perspectives. From the church, the tour continues along the southern path to the Mount of Flora, a small hill bearing a statue of the goddess of flowers (by

Interior of the Church of Peace. Watercolour by Carl Graeb.

Albert Wolff, before 1850) as well as a blossom-shaped flower bed. At the end of the path, two former gardeners' houses from the 18th century can be seen. From here, the visitor can savour a wonderful view: the vineyard rising up, with Sans Souci Palace framed between two playful sphinxes (1755, by Georg Franz Ebenhech). The tour ends at the palace.

Dragon House.

Sans Souci Park: Tour 2
From the Historic Mill to the
Chinese Tea House

The tour begins at the **Historic Mill**, the windmill of the legendary Miller of Sans Souci. The wooden upper part was hit by a phosphor shell in 1945 and burnt down. Reconstuction lasted for many years but was completed in time for Potsdam's millennium jubilee in 1993. A flour-mill museum has been set up inside.

Many tales are woven about the mill and its miller. His name was Grävenitz and he is said to have opposed Frederick the Great, who had threatened to remove the mill because its clattering bothered him. The Supreme Court in Berlin upheld the miller's claim and he was allowed to keep his mill. This story is often retold to emphasize the rule of law during the reign of Frederick the Great. In reality, though, Frederick probably never objected to the mill, which formed a charming backdrop for his guests' palace, the New Chambers.

Across the road, a few steps beyond the former royal stables, the visitor finds an inn named after the Historic Mill *(Historische Mühle)*. Erected in 1909, the inn bears witness to Potsdam's popularity for holiday excursions as early as the beginning of the 20th century.

The tour now leads a short way along the street *An der Orangerie*, then turns left into the *Lindenallee*. Within just a few steps, the dense plant growth along the avenue opens up and the visitor comes to a terrace. Directly below, two small, enclosed gardens are visible: the Nordic Garden and the Sicilian Garden (laid out between 1857 and 1860 by Peter Joseph Lenné). The two form a complementary pair. The Nordic Garden with its many conifers has a dark, serious atmosphere, in contrast to the bright, serene Sicilian Garden, which is characterized by palms, agaves and other potted plants as well as by colourful summer flowers. The two gardens were meant to form a part of a vast triumphal avenue planned by King Frederick William IV as a memorial to Frederick the Great.

41

The avenue was to begin at the *Winzerberg*, a vineyard which was situated behind the triumphal gate in the *Schopenhauerstrasse* near the Obelisk (see page 35). From there, the avenue would have continued over a viaduct to Sans Souci Palace, then past the Historic Mill to the Nordic Garden, where a casino was also planned. Just a few parts of the project were realized. The only larger building completed was the **Orangery Palace**, built between 1850 and 1864 from designs by Ludwig Persius (1803–1845), Friedrich August Stüler (1800–1865) and Ludwig Ferdinand Hesse (1795–1876). From the Nordic garden, the visitor follows the *Lindenallee* to reach the Orangery Palace. Its imposing, 300-metre-long south façade appears quite Mediterranean in summer when the large potted plants are outside. In the winter months, the plants are kept in the western wintering hall. The eastern one is currently used by the Brandenburg State Central Archive. Italian Renaissance models are evident in many details of the Orangery: the central building with its twin towers, for example, resembles the Villa Medici in Rome. Frederick William IV was an enthusiastic admirer of Italian architecture, which he had encountered during travels

Sicilian Garden.

Orangery Palace.

in Italy. The king, whose statue (1873, by Gustav Bläser, 1813–1874) stands in front of the central building, had a decisive influence on the planning of the Orangery. In the niches beside the statue are sculptures representing (from left to right) Gardening, Architecture, Industry and Science. Similar figures adorn the garden side of the Picture Gallery as well (see page 33), but here, a century later, the group is joined by the somewhat strange allegory of Industry in the shape of a woman lost in contemplation of a gear. The statues on the façade of the wintering halls are thematically related to the building's function as an orangery: they represent the months and the seasons.

A beautiful picture gallery, the Raphael Room, is found inside the central building. Here, too, the Italian Renaissance influence is clear. The room was inspired by the Sala Regia in the Vatican and the paintings, placed here at the wish of Frederick William IV, are copies of works by Raphael. Like the Church of Peace (see page 38), this room, the Orangery and the whole triumphal avenue project were opportunities for the king to flee from the pressing tasks of his time into artistic spheres. The Guest Rooms which adjoin the Raphael Room form a singular contrast to the light garden façade.

View of Potente's Plot.

Decorated in a style called the second Rococo, these rooms were intended as apartments for the Russian Czar Nicholas I and his consort during their visits in Potsdam (the czarina was one of Frederick William IV's sisters). To the visitor of today, the cold splendour of these rooms conveys a strange impression: they feel more like a museum than a dwelling.

The view from the tower platform of the Orangery, extending over the entire park as far as the city, calls the visitor back into the present. To the North is Bornstedt. The church, designed in the Italian style by August Stüler (1800–1865) and built in 1855/56, is distinctly visible. Peter Joseph Lenné is buried in the cemetery there, as are many other architects and gardeners who worked in Sans Souci. A detour to the Bornstedt cemetery is a must for visitors who have enough time.

Greenhouse in the Botanical Garden.

The avenue was intended to lead through the arches of the corner pavilions at both ends of the Orangery, then continue westward, and finally end at the Belvedere on the *Klausberg*. This palace is situated at the end of the *Lindenallee*, along which the tour continues. The garden parcel crossed now is commonly called Potente's Plot, after the Director of Gardens Georg Potente (1876–1945), who laid out this garden between 1904 and 1908 at the behest of Emperor William II. The Emperor was a great lover of Scandinavia and wanted here to be reminded of the Nordic countryside.

The Paradise Garden, laid out by Lenné in 1844 and adorned with a fountain house built by Ludwig Persius following ancient models, is found to the south of Potente's Plot. The Potsdam University redesigned the Paradise Garden for study purposes and still uses it today.

The **Belvedere** atop the *Klausberg* is currently undergoing restoration. This palace (1770–1772, by Georg Christian Unger) marks the end of Frederick the Great's building activity in Sans Souci. One feels as though the king wanted the Belvedere to be a lookout point commanding a total view of the buildings and the garden landscape created during his reign. The two-storey, circular edifice is surrounded by an open hypostyle and crowned with a low dome. Outside, a curved double stairway leads to the upper floor. Inside were two round halls, placed one above the other. During the fighting around Potsdam in April of 1945, however, the Belvedere burnt as a result of artillery fire, leaving only the external walls standing. Reconstruction began in 1990, and the exterior works should be completed in 1995.

Frederick the Great had the hillside in front of the Belvedere laid out as a vineyard, of which only a few traces remain. The wine-grower who worked the vineyard lived in the nearby **Dragon House** (1770, by Karl von Gontard). This small building, styled after a pagoda, is named for the gilded embossed copper dragons on the upswept corners of the eaves. Today it serves as a café. The

Sculpture group at the Chinese Tea House.

Chinese Tea House.

Dragon House owes its origin to the *chinoiserie* fashion widespread in the court art of the 18th century. It became customary to collect porcelain and other works of art from the far East, and soon whole rooms were decorated in Chinese style – the first guest room in Sans Souci Palace is an example. The delicate shapes of East Asian art were soon incorporated in the playful rococo ornamentation. Examples of *chinoiserie* compositions more famous than the Dragon House include the Chinese Tea House and Pillnitz Palace near Dresden.

A stair leads down from the Dragon House to the *Maulbeerallee*. The name of this street, meaning »Mulberry Avenue« in English, refers to Frederick the Great's efforts to promote domestic crafts. The king wanted in particular to develop the silk industry in order to save the expense of importing raw silk. For this reason, great mulberry plantations were laid out in the environs of Potsdam. But the enterprise soon had to be abandoned, as the natural conditions necessary for raising silkworms were not present.

After crossing the *Maulbeerallee*, the tour leads eastward a short way. But first, the visitor should take time to make a detour of a few

47

New Chambers, garden side.

48

paces through the narrow gate in the wrought-iron fence to a small mound to the right of the path. This was the princes' playground. For his sons' military training, Emperor William II (1859–1941) had a miniature fortification constructed here, parts of which are still distinguishable. The fittings of the fortress included small cannons made by the Krupp company.

Back to the *Maulbeerallee*: on his right, the visitor soon sees a gateway which leads back into Sans Souci Park. The tour continues along the **Botanical Garden** of the Potsdam University. The greenhouses shelter an interesting assortment of plants from tropical and subtropical areas. A rich collection of orchids is found here, as well as useful plants such as coffee, pepper, pineapples, bananas, cocoa, cinnamon, figs, etc.

After passing the greenhouses, the visitor walks through a shady wooded patch and suddenly arrives at a wide garden area belonging to the Orangery. The centre of this area is occupied by a parterre composed of a large, slightly sunken lawn bordered by trimmed hedges. Benches are set in the half-round niches formed by the hedges. The parterre was laid out in 1913 for the twenty-fifth jubilee of Emperor William II. At the north end of the parterre, below the *Maulbeerallee*, the Jubilee Terrace and the fountain basin, with the open hall behind it, were built for the same occasion. The terrace was cunningly added to the Orangery gardens already laid out by Lenné, creating an almost imperceptible transition. Lenné had modelled his design after Italian Renaissance gardens. After his death in 1866, the works were suspended, so that the grounds were never completely finished. Seen from here, the central building of the Orangery with its twin towers is quite imposing. Originally, the Orangery was planned as just part of the independent project for the triumphal avenue which was to run parallel to Sans Souci Park. The parterre laid out in 1913, however, highlights the visual effect of the Orangery and its balanced architecture at a greater distance, and integrates the palace in the park. At the southern end of the parterre stands a marble equestrian statue of Frederick the Great. It is a smaller copy of the bronze sculpture by Christian Daniel Rauch (1777–1857) found in the boulevard *Unter den Linden* in Berlin.

After leaving the Orangery parterre, the visitor comes to a circle in the main avenue. At the western end of the avenue, the imposing New Palace (see page 59) can be seen. In the circle are eight sandstone sculptures representing figures from classical mythology. The area around the circle is called the Deer Garden. Even in the 18th century, this area was far less intensively styled than, for example, the parcels around Sans Souci Palace. It was in large part

New Chambers, Ovid Gallery.

Lenné's remodelling in the 19th century that gave the Deer Garden the character it has today. On the main avenue, not far from the Orangery circle, a marble colonnade erected after 1751 by Georg Wenzeslaus von Knobelsdorff once stood. This construction, marking the centre of the Deer Garden, featured a richly sculpted, partially gilded ornamentation. It also constituted a pleasing break in the great length of the main avenue extending toward the New Palace.

Through an opening in the hedge surrounding the Orangery circle, the visitor can see the **Chinese Tea House**, the next stop on the tour. After a few steps along the main avenue, the visitor turns right onto the asphalted path leading to the Tea House. This building was erected between 1754 and 1757 from designs by Johann Gottfried Büring, who was also the architect of the Picture Gallery.

New Chambers, Jasper Hall.

The Chinese Tea House was likewise commissioned by Frederick the Great.

This pavilion appears fantastic and at the same time mysterious. Delight in the exotic and a taste for rich ornamentation, both typical of rococo art, are here combined in a fascinating way. Like the Neptune Grotto (see page 35), the Chinese Tea House is primarily an example of garden architecture, a charming decoration for the garden; but this building was also a setting for small gatherings. Nature and Art, open space and architecture are bound together here in a harmonious whole. The ground plan of the Tea House has the shape of a clover leaf. A circular inner room widens out in regular intervals to three leaf-shaped chambers, which correspond to

New Chambers, Marquetry Room.

three open spaces in the garden. Porticos are placed between the exterior projections formed by the chambers. Here another stylized form from nature is found: the roofs of the porticos are carried by gilded sandstone palms. The sculpture groups placed around the palms are also gilded, as are the statues of Chinese musicians standing in front of the chambers. One almost feels transported into an Oriental fairy tale. The beautiful contrast between the gold and the green of nature heightens the magical effect of the scene. On the lawn in front of the Chinese Tea House an East Asian incense burner has been placed.

The fresco on the ceiling of the central room reproduces the theme of the sculpture group outside. The painter, Thomas Huber,

has depicted a leisurely gathering of Chinese seen behind a balustrade. Between its columns hang garlands on which monkeys swing while parrots fly here and there. Not far from the Tea House, but on the other side of the small canal, stands the kitchen with its hexagonal windows.

Continuing north-east, the visitor comes to the Hedge Garden. Here the path is lined with high hedges trimmed to form walls. In comparison with the Deer Garden, this parcel appears quite baroque, even if its paths and hedged plots do not show the typically baroque orientation with respect to the palace. In the 18th century, the plots were planted with fruits and vegetables. But today, there is a thick growth of trees in the Hedge Garden. Unfortunately, the hedges have been heavily damaged by pests in recent years. Some have been replanted, and now patience is called for until they grow to maturity. The centre of the Hedge Garden is the Circle of the Muses, which is crossed by the main avenue. In keeping with traditional French garden design, eight paths lead out from here in a star. Likewise eight sculptures (works of Friedrich Christian Glume) adorn this circle, representing the Muses, the ancient goddesses of the arts and sciences. Clockwise beginning with the figure to the left of the path toward the New Palace, they are: Thalia (comedy), Melpomene (tragedy), Erato (lyric poetry), Clio (history), Polymnia (sacred song), Calliope (epic poetry), Terpsichore (dance) and Euterpe (erotic poetry).

The visitor leaves the Circle of the Muses to go north toward the Rock Gate, which forms the counterpart to the Neptune Grotto situated on the other side of the Sans Souci hill. After a short halt at the Corradini vase, the tour will continue to the left toward the Sicilian Garden. The vase is loosely copied from the famous ornamental marble vase which formerly stood in the Great Garden in Dresden and was a work by the Italian Antonio Corradini. The bas-relief frieze on the vase shows Alexander the Great and the women captured from Darius. The sculptures in the round are particularly interesting: Sensuality, in the shape of a winged female figure, is portrayed triumphing over Innocence.

But the visitor is soon captivated by the lively beauty of the **Sicilian Garden**. The colourful summer flowers and the potted plants from the Orangery – including date palms, dwarf palms and agaves – create a pleasant, Mediterranean atmosphere.

The tour is completed with a visit to one more palace, the **New Chambers**. Lying to the East above the Sicilian Garden, this palace attracts far too few visitors' attention. But the interior designs of the New Chambers, which served as Frederick the Great's guest

54

Frederick William IV. Statue by Gustav Bläser.

View toward the Historic Mill. Photograph taken before 1945.

56

house, are well worth seeing. Four remarkable banquet halls and seven guest rooms are found here. This building's modestly styled façade makes the effect of its interiors all the more surprising as one great, bright hall follows another.

Probably the most outstanding of these is the Jasper Hall, situated under the cupola. Dark red jasper and white marble adorn the walls and the floor. Gilded consoles supporting marble busts create a striking contrast to the red jasper. The visitor will find the adjoining Ovid Gallery much more serene. Large mirrors face the windows and give the gold and green hall an illusion of greater spaciousness. These interiors date from the remodelling conducted between 1771 and 1774 by Georg Christian Unger (1743–1806). Erected in 1747 by Georg Wenzeslaus von Knobelsdorff, the building was originally an orangery. Today, the large south windows and the ramps for transporting potted plants are reminders of this earlier function. The room decorations created in the course of the remodelling exude once more the whole beauty of Friderician Rococo. A general restoration performed a few years ago by Polish specialists gave the rooms new splendor.

The exterior of the New Chambers was also decisively altered by Unger's remodelling. This architect added the cupola, matching the building's appearance to that of the Picture Gallery (see page 33). Even today, the result is impressive. A complete, symmetrical architectural ensemble was created, with Sans Souci Palace in the centre, flanked by two similar buildings.

The Historic Mill, situated behind the New Chambers, offers an admirable contrast to this ensemble. The tour ends at the Mill.

Eagle crest of Brandenburg on a side cupola of the New Palace.

58

Sans Souci Park: Tour 3
From the New Palace to
Charlottenhof Palace

The third tour through Sans Souci Park begins at the **New Palace**, situated at the west end of the main avenue which runs in a straight line through the entire length of Sans Souci Park. The New Palace appears quite imposing and captivating as the visitor approaches it from the south. On the right is the palace proper, a three-winged building with two supplementary lateral wings, and on the left, opposite the New Palace, are the two household wings called the *Communs*, linked by a colonnade. Considering their very elaborate styling, it is hard to believe that the *Communs* were merely outbuildings. The entire complex was built in the surprisingly short time of six years, between 1763 and 1769. Three architects were involved in the project: Johann Gottfried Büring (1723–1766), Heinrich Ludwig Manger (1728–1790), and Karl von Gontard (1731–1791). In 1763, the year construction began, the Treaty of Hubertusburg was signed, marking the end of the Seven Years' War. Devastating for all sides, this war had brought the country to the brink of ruin, but the terms of the peace treaty left no doubt: Prussia emerged as a great power in Europe. Frederick the Great sought here to reflect in architecture the Prussian state's increase in power. The building is one of superlatives: it is 220 metres long and over 400 sculptures adorn the façade. The interior is splendidly decorated. Frederick himself described the New Palace as *fanfaronnade*, as bragging. After the works were completed, the king never developed a real liking for the building. Frederick rarely resided at the New Palace, preferring his »old« Sans Souci Palace.

With its symmetrical three-winged structure completed by two lateral wings, the main building at first appears thoroughly baroque. The majestic effect is accentuated by a mighty dome, on top of which the three Graces stand, bearing the royal crown of Prussia. The smaller cupolas of the lateral wings, crowned with gilded eagles, echo the dome motif of the central building. A closer look reveals that the New Palace lacks a typical element of the baroque

59

style: there is no stairway leading to regal apartments on the first floor. In fact, the king's apartments are not situated in the centre of the building – a further breach with baroque architectural tradition–, but in one of the lateral wings. These deviations from conventional style are due primarily to the personal wishes of the architects' royal patron. One must bear in mind, however, that other parts of Europe had long been building in Classic styles, while the King of Prussia remained true until his death to the traditional forms of Baroque and Rococo. Even today, the classification and evaluation of this – nonetheless grandiose – architectural ensemble presents a problem for art historians.

The *Communs*, the household wings opposite the New Palace, seem like a fantastic stage backdrop. It appears more than curious that these majestic buildings with colonnades and great, double exterior stairways housed the kitchens, and that servants lived behind these regal façades. Architectural considerations necessitated the elaborate form: the immense edifice of the New Palace needed a balancing counterpart and an attractive optical complement.

At present, the New Palace and the *Communs* are undergoing large- scale restoration work. Not only the façade of the palace and the colonnades between the *Communs*, but also the southern cupola of the *Communs*, which burnt in World War II, must be restored. In the course of work on the façade, the sandstone sculptures will also be restored. Over the centuries, many of these have taken on a dark, almost black colour. This crust will not be removed, however: it acts as a protective shield against caustic agents in the environment. Only severely damaged sculptures will be stored away and replaced with copies.

The New Palace was meant to be a summer residence for members of the royal family and their guests. The arrangement of the rooms follows from this purpose. In the centre of the building are four banquet halls, two on the ground floor and two on the first floor. Adjoining the halls on both sides are splendid princely apartments, whose antechambers are furnished as picture galleries. Coming from the forecourt, the visitor enters the palace through the central door and arrives in the Lower Vestibule. This room, structured by pairs of columns, follows the example set by the Vestibule in Sans Souci Palace (see page 24). The ceiling painting by Johann Christoph Frisch (1738–1815) shows Apollo, the god of the Arts, with the Muses already encountered at the circle named for them in the main avenue.

The next room is the famous Grotto or Shell Room. It served as a garden room. Looking through the middle window, the visitor can

New Palace, Grotto Room.

New Palace, garden side.

New Palace, Theatre.

observe the axial alignment of the New Palace with the main avenue. The grotto motif also occurs at the opposite end of the main avenue, where the Neptune Grotto is found (see page 35). The walls of the Grotto Room are decorated with shells, minerals, coral and glass slag. The precious gems and fossils were added during the time of the German Empire, for the New Palace was an imperial residence until 1918. As a result of the growing demands of comfort, electric lighting, steam heating and a lift were installed at the end of the 19th century. Several of the wardrobes were converted into bathrooms, one of which can be seen during the tour of the palace.

Leaving the dark depths of the marine world behind in the Grotto Room, the visitor enters the bright Marble Gallery, which conveys an emphatically festive mood. Red jasper and white Carrara marble dominate here. Large mirrors opposite the windows connect the room with the surrounding nature. The three-part ceiling painting by Christian Bernhard Rode (1725–1797) allegorically depicts Morning, Noon and Night. On the first floor, directly above the Grotto Room, is the largest room in the palace, the Mar-

New Palace, Marble Hall.

ble Hall. This banquet room is embellished with large illustrations of scenes from classical mythology, works by French 18th-century painters. In the ceiling painting by Charles Amedée Philippe van Loo, the Olympian gods are shown gathered for a meal. The next room, the Upper Gallery, is one of the most interesting specimens of interior design in the New Palace. Many details in this room dominated by muted colours already hint at Classicism, while the six paintings which form part of the wall decoration are considered masterpieces of Italian baroque painting.

In addition to the ballrooms and princely apartments, the New Palace also contains a theatre, situated in the south wing, above the Palace Café. The theatre is not just a place to visit as one of the most beautiful examples of German Rococo but is also regularly used for operas, plays and concerts.

After the majestic architectural ensemble of the New Palace, the quiet scenery of **Charlottenhof Park**, the next destination on this tour, seems suddenly to transport the visitor into another world. Charlottenhof is reached by walking a short way along the *Ökono-mieweg*, an asphalted path leading east from the south end of the

New Palace. Soon the path crosses a circular hedged plot where Apollo and Diana stand, bronze copies of two ancient marble statues. The visitor turns right a few steps beyond the statues. The garden that comes into view here makes a completely different impression from that of the geometrical lawns, flower beds and hedges in the old Friderician gardens. Created after 1826, Charlottenhof Park is a landscape garden corresponding to the aesthetics of that time. This type of garden had already spread from England to the rest of Europe by the middle of the 18th century. In contrast to the baroque garden, whose design is orientated toward the palace as a central point, the landscape garden is composed of diverse design elements coexisting in equality and harmony. The basic elements are trees, meadows and water, with sculptures, buildings and monuments to complete the scenery. Charlottenhof is no exception: wide expanses of meadow, accented by small woods, give this garden its character. The ordering hand of man is to remain invisible as far as possible. The park appears as a natural, but ideal landscape. The clever arrangement of trees, copses and shrubs creates long vistas through the park; small buildings appearing in the distance catch the eye. From the »Drive,« as the main road around the park is called, changing, ever surprising views of this garden can be discovered.

View of the New Palace from Charlottenhof Palace.

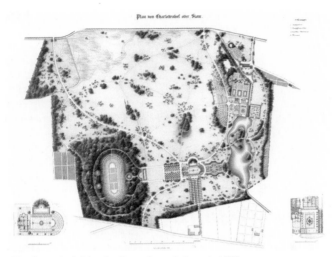

Charlottenhof. Plan by Peter Joseph Lenné, 1839.

The creation of Charlottenhof extended Sans Souci Park to the south-west by an area of approximately one square kilometre, thus improving the proportions of the park, which had been stretched along the east-west axis. The idea for this extension dates back to the late 18th century, but not until 1825 did King Frederick William III decide to purchase the land in question. The king made a gift of the land to his eldest son, the crown prince Frederick William (who succeeded to the throne in 1840 as Frederick William IV), so that he might build here a summer house and garden for himself and his consort Elizabeth. The crown prince was artistically interested and talented to an extraordinary degree. Having travelled in Italy, he was especially enthusiastic about Italian architecture and the Italian countryside. He had two artists at his disposal, Peter Joseph Lenné (1789–1866) and Karl Friedrich Schinkel (1781–1841). Both were able to execute the crown prince's ideas with understanding and creativity. While Lenné was responsible for laying out the garden, Schinkel was commissioned to design the buildings. Charlottenhof is an example of the two artists' successful cooperation.

Following the gently curved path, the visitor soon discovers the Fasanerie (1842–1844, by Ludwig Persius; here pheasants were kept in a fenced area in the 19th century). Also visible is the Temple of Friendship, which will be visited later in the tour. Again and

67

Charlottenhof Palace, Living Room.

again, smaller paths branch off to the left into the park, although the eye cannot follow their course, since they lie below the level of the meadow. The meadows therefore appear unbroken. Following the main path, the visitor comes to **Charlottenhof Palace**, built by Schinkel between 1826 and 1829 as a summer residence for the crown prince and his consort. The palace was created by remodelling an old country house which had been owned by one Marie Charlotte von Gentzkow, whence the name of Charlottenhof. Simple, smooth forms characterize the palace's exterior design. This building exemplifies Schinkel's mastery of classical architecture. And yet he had to keep his plans within narrow financial limits: one consequence was the conservation of the original ground plan of the country house. That fact makes the great number of rooms and their well-conceived arrangement all the more astonishing. Only in the bedroom did Schinkel deviate from the existing ground plan to add a semicircular projection. The views from the windows of this projection contribute to the harmonious unity of palace and garden. The room furnishings have been almost completely preserved and convey a detailed picture of the living conditions of the crown prince and his consort. In contrast to the 18th-century palaces in Sans Souci, Charlottenhof was built with indoor toilets. Baths were

Charlottenhof Palace, Dining Room.

present only in Glienicke Palace, built at the same time for Prince Charles. Compared with the splendour of the New Palace, Charlottenhof seems rather like a well-furnished middle-class home. What a change occurred in the fifty years that separate the construction dates of the two palaces!

The tour continues outside on the terrace behind the palace. This elevated point affords particularly beautiful views far into the park. The terrace ends in an exedra, a semicircular marble bench, below which a flower garden extends out to an artificial pond called the *Maschinenteich*. At the edge of this garden, on the pond's shore, stands a large marble basin marking the site of the pump house that once supplied the fountains in Charlottenhof Park. The name of the pond is derived from the steam machinery in the pump house. The installation became obsolete and was demolished after the construction of the »mosque« on the Neustadt Bay of the Havel (see page 22).

The tour follows the shore of the pond northward – offering an opportunity to make a detour to the island, with its statue of Germanicus Cæsar atop a tall column. After a while, the visitor arrives at the buildings of the **Roman Baths** (erected 1829–1840, from plans by Karl Friedrich Schinkel). This ensemble, already visible

from the terrace of Charlottenhof Palace, appears thoroughly Italian. The design of the front is clearly inspired by Italian country houses. In the larger house, whose tower forms a vertical extension the court gardener responsible for Charlottenhof had his abode, while the smaller house was for his assistant. Walking through the inner courtyard, where plots of artichokes, hemp, tobacco and maize accentuate the southern character of the site, the visitor reaches the bath, which is of ancient Roman inspiration. The bath building, which gave the ensemble its name, never really fulfilled its function, but served the crown prince rather as a sort of museum, a place to reflect upon memories of Italy.

In front of the Roman Baths, at a fork in the path, stands a sandstone sundial, erected here in 1834. The right-hand path, bordered by dark conifers, leads to the Dairy (1833–1834, by Ludwig Persius), also built in keeping with Italian forms. But following the left-hand path, the visitor meets up with the *Ökonomieweg*, which once more offers a view of the broad garden expanses of Charlottenhof Park. After walking for a while along the asphalted path, the visitor discovers the **Temple of Friendship** (1768 –1770, by Karl von Gontard). This round pavilion, currently undergoing restoration, was dedicated by Frederick the Great to his favorite sister, Wilhelmine. Here, the tour leaves the *Ökonomieweg* and follows the narrow, winding paths leading past the temple. The visitor sudden-

Flower Garden at Charlottenhof Palace.

Roman Baths.

ly comes to the main avenue and finds himself in front of the imposing garden-side façade of the New Palace, before a sweeping semicircular parterre, bordered by a path running between rows of chestnut trees. Here the visitor keeps to the right along the path under the shade of the chestnut trees. The next branching path leads to a densely wooded parcel, where the counterpart to the Temple of Friendship, the **Ancient Temple** (1768–1769, also by Karl von Gontard), is found. The outer form of this building imitates the Pantheon in Rome. Frederick the Great kept a part of his collection of ancient statues and busts here. After the Old Museum in Berlin was erected in 1830, the sculptures were moved there. The Ancient Temple became a mausoleum in 1921, when Empress Augusta Victoria (1858–1921), the consort of William II, was buried here. Later, other members of the imperial family were also laid to eternal rest here. From the temple, it is only a short way back to the New Palace, where the tour ends.

Roman Baths, Caldarium.

Detour: Lindstedt Palace

Going north along the path parallel to the garden side of the New Palace, the visitor reaches **Lindstedt Palace** in about fifteen minutes. The path leaves Sans Souci Park through the beautiful wrought iron Lindstedt Gate, which is about the halfway point. Lindstedt Palace was built from designs by the architects L. Persius, L. F. Hesse, F. A. Stüler and F. von Arnim. After nearly twenty years of planning, the palace was finally constructed from 1859 to 1860 by L. F. Hesse. Although this late classical villa was intended as a residence for Frederick William IV in his old age, the king did not live here, for he died in 1861.

The recently restored garden was laid out by P. J. Lenné. Today the palace houses the administration of the Brandenburg State Institute for Forensic Medicine.

Sketches by Frederick William IV largely determined the different designs which were envisaged for the palace. Over the years,

72

Ancient Temple.

the king changed his mind several times: his ambitions were gradually reduced from a palatial construction, generous both in ground plan and in elevation (twin towers were planned), to a gracious, romantic-classical villa similar to those characterizing Potsdam's suburbs since the first half of the 19th century.

But the little palace distinguishes itself from other villas through its sumptuous, lovingly executed architectural details. The tower, the colonnade and the perron with portico closely connect the house with the garden and the surrounding landscape. The park was originally much larger.

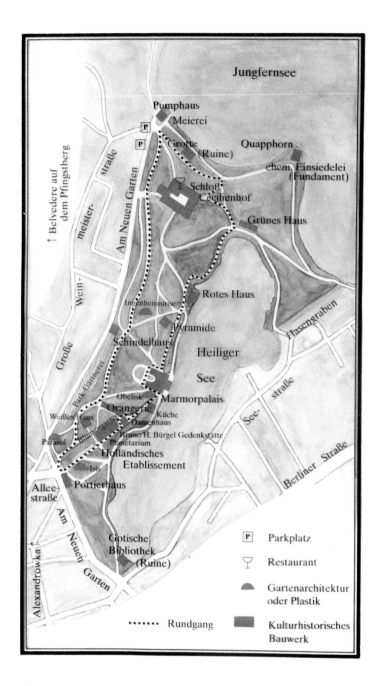

Jungfernsee

Pumphaus

Meierei

P

P

Grotte
(Ruine)

Quapphorn

ehem. Einsiedelei
(Fundament)

↑ Belvedere auf
dem Pfingstberg

Schloß
Cecilienhof

Grünes Haus

straße

meister-

Am Neuen Garten

Wein-

Rotes Haus

Ingenheimurne

Große

Pyramide

Schindelhaus

Heiliger

See

Hasengraben

Park-Gärtnerei

Obelisk

Orangerie

Marmorpalais

See-

straße

Weißes Haus

Küche

Damenhaus

Blumengärtnerei

Bruno H. Bürgel Gedenkstätte

Planetarium

Parasol

Holländisches

Etablissement

Berliner Straße

Isis

Portierhaus

Allee-
straße

Am

Neuen

Gotische
Bibliothek
(Ruine)

Garten

Alexandrowka

P   Parkplatz

Ⴗ   Restaurant

◖   Gartenarchitektur
oder Plastik

•••••• Rundgang

█   Kulturhistorisches
Bauwerk

74

The New Garden
From the Marble Palace to Cecilienhof Palace

Dutch Houses • Orangery • Marble Palace
Cecilienhof Palace • Dairy
Detour: Russian Colony of Alexandrovka
and Belvedere on the »Pfingstberg«

The New Garden, situated north of the city on the shore of the *Heiliger See*, was laid out after Sans Souci Park, under the reign of King Frederick William II (1741–1797). This monarch, Frederick the Great's successor, ushered in a new aesthetics in Prussia. He was open to Classicism, which was becoming the dominant architectural style, and was an enthusiastic supporter of the new trend in garden design, the landscape garden. To lay out the New Garden – new in relation to Sans Souci –, Frederick William engaged Johann August Eyserbeck (1762–1801), a native of Wörlitz. The choice of this garden designer was influenced by Frederick William's personal acquaintance with the beauty of the landscape park at Wörlitz near Dessau. And the king's mistress Wilhelmine Encke, who was a counsellor to him in artistic matters, was also from that area.

Between 1787 and 1793, Eyserbeck built a sentimental landscape garden with picturesque scenery accented by ornamental buildings. Diverse historical styles were made use of in designing these buildings, the most important criterion being an appealing visual effect. The kitchen building of the Marble Palace was built in the form of a half-sunken ruined temple, and the ice house took the shape of a pyramid. A »Gothic« library was built, as well as a »Norman« dairy.

Several of the wine-growers' houses that had stood in the vineyards which once occupied the site of the New Garden were integrated into the landscape design and are now called the Red, Green, White and Brown Houses, according to their respective paint colours.

Peter Joseph Lenné (1789–1866) redesigned the New Garden after 1817, and eliminated the patchwork effect that had arisen

The tour route is marked on the map on the facing page.

through the acquisition of the land in irregular parcels. He created generous perspectives, bringing about an impression of wide spaces and making one forget the limited width of the garden. Through visual contacts with the park on the Peacock Island and those in Sacrow, Nikolskoe, Glienicke and Babelsberg, Lenné integrated the New Garden in his »plan for the embellishment of the environs of Potsdam.«

The tour begins at the main entrance, flanked by red gatehouses, to be found at the eastern end of the *Allee-Strasse*. A gravelled avenue running between conical-shaped oaks starts here and leads straight to the Marble Palace. A row of **Dutch Houses** (1789–1790, by Karl von Gontard) which accomodated servants lines the left side of the avenue. This type of house had been known in Potsdam since the construction of the Dutch Quarter in the 1730s. Opposite the houses, a meadow slopes gently down to the shore of the *Heiliger See*. In the middle of this meadow, in a thicket of white pines, stands a statue of Isis, a symbol of Mother Nature and Immortality according to the iconography of the Rosicrucian order, with which Frederick William II was associated. Ladies-in-waiting used to live in the last of the Dutch houses, the Ladies' House, behind which the visitor finds the elongated **Orangery** (1791–1793, by Carl Gotthard Langhans). This building has an end wall ornamented with Egyptian motifs and large windows opening on the south.

The colourful flower garden with its imaginatively shaped conifers is enlivened by two fountains, whose ornamental figures were created by Gerhard Lichtenfeld (1921–1978). The tour continues toward the Marble Palace, which is soon announced by a marble obelisk (by Karl von Gontard) decorated with four medallions (by Johann Gottfried Schadow and the Wohler brothers) symbolizing the four seasons.

Frederick William II had the **Marble Palace** built as a summer residence between 1787 and 1791 by the architects Karl von Gontard (1731–1791) and Carl Gotthard Langhans (1732–1808). First just the central building was erected, but later the side wings were added as the small ground plan proved insufficient. The construction was at first supervised by von Gontard, who was chiefly responsible for the exterior design. This artist had been in Frederick the Great's service since 1764 and in many details he still appears a proponent of late baroque architecture. Yet the simple structure and the harmonious proportions of the Marble Palace make this building a milestone of early classic architecture in Berlin and Potsdam.

King Frederick William II. Portrait by Anton Graff.

The Marble Palace was originally designed to be seen from the *Heiliger See*. It is reflected in the water's surface as a beautiful, almost visionary scene, framed between the pyramid and the half-sunken temple ruin that housed the kitchens (1788–1790, by von Gontard). Looking from the palace to the opposite shore, the visitor sees the villas of the *Berliner Vorstadt*, the suburb of Potsdam extending toward Berlin. Today, it is difficult to imagine the quiet isolated countryside of fields and meadows, interspersed with windmills, that was once found here. From the lakeside terrace of the Marble Palace, the visitor can see in the distance, at the edge of the New Garden, another building of equally remarkable design: the town palace of the Countess Lichtenau, located in the street now called *Behlertstrasse*.

Only the addition of the side wings, which were not completed until 1840, gave the Marble Palace a definitive orientation toward the garden. In front of the garden side, a luxuriant, richly coloured carpet of over forty kinds of flowers spreads out in summer. At pre-

77

The Ladies' House and the end wall of the orangery.

sent, the Marble Palace is a building site. A thorough restoration, which will take several years, was indeed necessary: in 1945 the house fell under Soviet administration and since 1961 it has been used, with utter disregard for its intended purpose, as an East German army museum. After restoration, the building will be reopened as a palace museum.

From the Marble Palace, the tour continues along the shore of the *Heiliger See* and further into the garden. Again and again, long vistas open up into the lake country around Potsdam, revealing Lenné's efforts to interconnect the most beautiful points in this landscape. Especially impressive is the view toward the Church of the Saviour in Sacrow – inspired, like the Church of Peace (see page 38), by Italian examples. The brilliant white façade of the palace on the Peacock Island is also visible in the distance. Soon the visitor passes by the pyramid (1791–1792, by Langhans) that originally served as an ice house.

Behind the pyramid, in a garden plot surrounded by tall trees, a white marble urn is found. It is a memorial to Countess Ingenheim, Frederick William II's wife by morganatic marriage, who died at an early age. The relief on the urn portrays a genius with a torch burning low to symbolize Death.

Flower garden in front of the Orangery.

The tour continues toward the Red House, formerly a wine-grower's house, which is situated on the edge of a small artificial bay. The hill beside it, called Rabbit Hill, was formed by piling up the earth removed in digging out the bay. Once again, the beautiful views of the garden and surrounding landscape tempt the visitor to pause on the hilltop.

But between the trees, the visitor can already discover the rustic looking façade of **Cecilienhof Palace**, characterized by its half-timbered elements. It was built from 1913 to 1917, after many designs had been drawn and then altered again. Cecilienhof Palace was intended for the Crown Prince William, son of Emperor William II, and named after his consort, the Crown Princess Cecilia. This palace, the last one built by the Hohenzollern dynasty, was designed by the architect Paul Schultze-Naumburg (1869–1949) following the style of an English country house. The artist cleverly structured the body of the palace so as to play down its real size and adapt it to the garden.

Cecilienhof Palace attained worldwide historical importance as the site of the Potsdam Conference. Lasting from July 17th until August 2nd, 1945, this conference was attended by the heads of government of the victorious Allies of World War II: Harry S. Tru-

*View across the Heiliger See toward the Marble Palace, the kitchens
and the pyramid.*

80

Cecilienhof Palace, Conference Room.

man, Joseph V. Stalin and Winston S. Churchill (the latter was replaced on July 28th, as a result of elections in Great Britain, by Clement R. Attlee, the new Prime Minister). Today, the conference room and the chambers of the American, Soviet and British delegations can be visited as a memorial. The remaining part of the palace functions as a hotel.

For almost three decades, the window of the conference room offered a view of the Berlin Wall, whose construction was an indirect consequence of the stipulations set down in the Potsdam Declaration. The wall was demolished in 1990, leaving a barren area of garden measuring about 14 hectares, which had to be recultivated at great expense.

On this terrain on the banks of the *Jungfernsee*, a lake formed by the Havel River, the visitor finds the ruins of two buildings: the Shell Grotto (1792–1794, by Andreas Ludwig Krüger), whose exterior formes an artificial cliff; and the Dairy (1791, by Carl Gotthard Langhans), which once resembled a castle. In 1844 Ludwig Persius converted the Dairy into a pump house to irrigate the New Garden.

The asphalt carriage drive running through the entire length of the New Garden offers a direct route back to the starting point, the gatehouses.

The half-timbered façade of Cecilienhof Palace.

Detour: Russian Colony of Alexandrovka and Belvedere
on the *Pfingstberg*

After the tour of the New Garden, an excursion to the **Russian colony of Alexandrovka**, north-west of the *Allee-Strasse*, is recommended. The thirteen log houses composing this settlement were built in 1826 to accomodate the members of a Russian military choir which had stayed with the Prussian army after the battles against Napoleon. On a hill near the houses is the Alexander Nevski Church, built for the colony. Potsdam's Russian Orthodox community still holds services here.

The path toward the **Belvedere on the Pfingstberg** climbs past the church and past the Jewish cemetery, consecrated in 1743. The vast palace building with its twin towers was built following Italian models and based on ideas by King Frederick William IV. Peter Joseph Lenné created perspectives connecting the palace on the Pfingstberg with other heights in and around Potsdam.

The Belvedere Palace is now merely a ruin. The small pavilion which stands in front of it, the so-called Temple of Pomona, was the first building designed by Karl Friedrich Schinkel. It was restored in 1992/93.

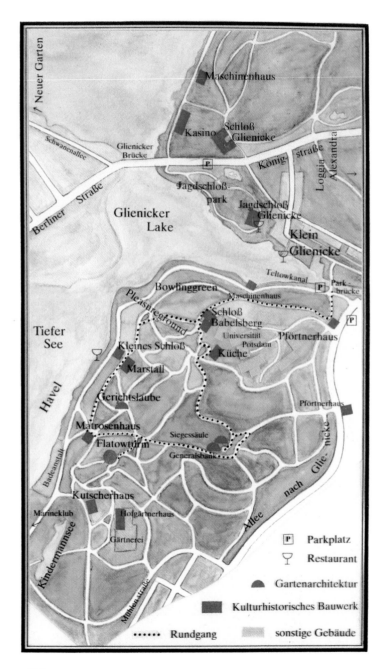

Neuer Garten

Maschinenhaus

Schwanenallee

Glienicker
Brücke

Kasino

Schloß
Glienicke

König-
straße

Loggia
Alexandra

Berliner
Straße

Jagdschloß-
park

Jagdschloß
Glienicke

Glienicker
Lake

Klein
Glienicke

Teltowkanal

Bowlinggreen

Maschinenhaus

Park-
brücke

P

Tiefer
See

Pleasureground

Schloß
Babelsberg

P

Pförtnerhaus

Kleines Schloß

Universität
Potsdam

Küche

Marstall

Havel

Gerichtslaube

Pförtnerhaus

Matrosenhaus

Siegessäule

Flatowturm

Generalsbank

nach Glie-
nicke

Kutscherhaus

Marineklub

Hofgärtnerhaus

Allee

P Parkplatz

Restaurant

Kindermannsee

Gärtnerei

Gartenarchitektur

Mühlen-straße

Kulturhistorisches Bauwerk

•••••• Rundgang

sonstige Gebäude

Babelsberg Park
From Babelsberg Palace
to the Flatow Tower

**Babelsberg Palace • Small Palace • Law Porch
Flatow Tower • Victory Column • Babelsberg Palace
Detour: Glienicke Palace Park**

The third great garden of Potsdam is Babelsberg Park. Situated on the rambling lakes of the Havel River on the east side of the city, this landscape park was laid out in several phases starting in 1832 as a summer residence for Prince William, later Emperor William I (1797–1888). It was Peter Joseph Lenné once again who, in the course of his landscape planning efforts, recommended purchasing the 44-metre-high *Babelsberg* for the purpose of transforming it into a garden. Lenné saw in this rolling terrain an ideal eastern boundary for his artistic landscaping projects in Potsdam and its environs. In 1843, Hermann von Pückler-Muskau (1785–1871) took over the project. This artist was already widely known for the park he had created in Muskau and for his book published in 1834, *Andeutungen über Landschaftsgärtnerei* (Notes on Landscape Gardening). Furthermore, von Pückler-Muskau's aesthetic notions corresponded more closely than Lenné's to those of Princess Augusta (1811–1890), William's consort, who exercised a decisive influence on the arrangement of Babelsberg. Von Pückler-Muskau retained the system of main roads created by Lenné, but added winding paths between them. Following these cunningly arranged paths, the visitor discovers again and again especially pleasing lookout points over the city and the countryside. After the death of William I, maintenance work in the Babelsberg gardens was drastically curtailed and shrubs and trees were allowed to grow unchecked. Gardeners here have been working for years carefully to recreate the original scenes and perspectives.

The tour begins at the end of the street *Allee nach Glienicke*, where the Park Bridge leads across the *Glienicker Lake* to Klein-Glienicke. Leaving the bridge behind to the right, the visitor follows the path leading gradually up the hillside. Soon the pump house appears on the right. This building, erected 1843–1845 by

The tour route is marked on the map on the facing page.

Emperor William I. Portrait by Paul Bülow.

Ludwig Persius, supplied water to the park's fountains and gardens. The structure of the building with its smokestack in the form of a tower reminds one of the »mosque,« the pump house on the Neustadt Bay of the Havel (see page 22). Like the New Garden, Babelsberg Park too lost part of its shoreline to the border fortifications of the Berlin Wall, in this case an area of almost 16 hectares extending as far as the palace. The pump house, which lay within this area, fell to ruins and now must be restored along with the recovered park land. Above the path are buildings of the former Academy for State and Law, an East German institution which spread out into the park with constructions that are quite out of place. Looking across the water, the visitor can enjoy an attractive view of the hunting seat at Glienicke, whose park is another of Lenné's designs. The view extends further to Glienicke Palace

Babelsberg Palace, Ballroom.

beyond the *Königstrasse*, so that all three parks converge visually to form a whole.

The path leads onward to **Babelsberg Palace**, the summer residence of Emperor William I. The first section of this purely Neo-Gothic building was executed in 1834/35 from designs by Karl Friedrich Schinkel. Because Prince William's demand for majestic appearances increased after he became crown prince in 1840, the palace was extended considerably in the following years by Ludwig Persius and Heinrich Strack (1805–1880). Since the demolition of the Berlin Wall, the visitor standing in front of the entrance side of the palace can see the Glienicker Bridge joining Berlin and Potsdam and enjoy a view already famous in the 19th century. Because the palace is still being used by the Brandenburg State Research Office for Pre- and Early History, only a few rooms can

Babelsberg Palace.

be visited. Through the entry hall at ground level, the visitor arrives in the tiled Vestibule, which is divided by pillars into nine areas. A stairway leads up to the first floor, where the tour of the palace starts with the antechamber, the parlour and the study of the Emperor's consort, Augusta. Pictures hung in the parlour give an idea of the original furnishings of the palace. Next comes the Tea Room with its restful, balanced proportions and its windows opening on to the beautiful garden. In the adjoining room the Library, the interesting ceiling design is unfortunately all that remains of the original decoration. The Ballroom, designed by Ludwig Persius, makes a stately impression. This octagonal hall, filling two storeys in height, is the largest room in the palace. A French window in the Ballroom leads out to the monument commemorating the Baden campaign of 1849, in which Prince William commanded the bloody suppression of a popular uprising. This campaign earned him the hardly honourable nick-name of »Shrapnel Prince.« The sculpture of the archangel Michael killing a dragon is by August Kiss (1802–1865). On the hillside above the palace is the kitchen building (1859–1860, by Rudolf Wilhelm Gottgetreu), which is connected with the palace by an underground passageway. Following the paths in the opposite direction, the visitor crosses the

»Pleasure Ground,« a flower garden sloping gently down to the Havel. This garden's intensive patchwork design, with its round flower beds, fountains and »Golden Rose Garden,« matches the richly structured façade of the palace.

The **Small Palace**, erected 1841–1842 by L. Persius, is seen to the right of the main path on the banks of the Havel. Ladies-in-waiting once lived here, but today a restaurant occupies the ground floor. Leaving this building behind, the visitor continues along the path that leads past the royal stables (1834–1839, by E. Gebhardt). From time to time, openings in the vegetation allow views of the city and of the Belvedere on the *Pfingstberg* (see page 83). To the left, red bricks soon shine through the green foliage of the trees. They are those of the medieval **Law Porch**. This building stood in the centre of Berlin from the 13th century until 1871, when it had to make way for the construction of the Red City Hall. The architecturally important parts of the structure were salvaged and the porch was moved to its present site. Below the Law Porch toward the Havel is the Sailors' House, with its extraordinary gables styled after those of the town hall in Stendal. Here were lodgings for the boatmen who sailed the boats kept at Babelsberg.

Law Porch.

View of the Flatow Tower.

Sailors' House.

On the hill opposite the Law Porch, the **Flatow Tower** rises up like a medieval moated castle, dominating the park. Modelled after the Eschenheim Gate in Frankfurt-on-Main, the tower was erected in 1853 on the site of an old windmill which had burnt down. The stones used for the building, and with them the tower's name, were brought from Flatow, Prince William's estate in West Prussia. Inside there is an exhibition of documents concerning the history of Babelsberg Park and one may also visit a small private room furnished in mid-19th century style. Since 1993, it is once more possible to look out from the platform.

The tour continues eastward, deeper into the park, through wooded areas. The path begins to climb again and after passing by the General's Bench, which William I had placed here in 1882, it ends on a hilltop with a particularly beautiful lookout point. The site is accentuated by the **Victory Column**, erected to commemorate Prussia's victory over Austria in 1866. The Victory goddess atop the column was sculpted by C. D. Rauch (1777–1857).

Victory column.

The way back leads first along the asphalted *Ökonomieweg*, then right toward the palace, which is near the starting point of the tour.

Detour: Glienicke Palace Park

Those who still feel energetic after the tour of Babelsberg Park should not miss the opportunity to take a walk (about 20 min.) to **Glienicke Palace Park**. The Italian-style park was designed for Prince Charles (1801–1883) after 1824 by Lenné in cooperation with Schinkel.

Tourist Information
How to Get There

Sans Souci Park
• Arrival at the station »Potsdam-Stadt« (national and local trains):
– Take tram 91 in the direction of »Schloss Charlottenhof« or tram 96 in the direction of »Bahnhof Pirschheide« (form. Hauptbahnhof) to »Luisenplatz«; walk from there to »Grünes Gitter« park entrance.
– Take tram 91 to »Schloss Charlottenhof« then walk to »Schloss Charlottenhof/Römische Bäder« park entrance.
– Take bus 695 to »Hermann-Elflein-Str./Luisenplatz«.
– In summer, take bus A 1 in the direction of Charlottenhof (the bus goes round Sans Souci Park).
• Arrival at »Potsdam-Busbahnhof« (coach station) at Bassinplatz:
– Take bus 695 in the direction of »Bahnhof Pirschheide« (form. Hauptbahnhof) to »Luisenplatz«, »Schloss Sanssouci«, »Orangerie« or »Neues Palais«.
– Walk about 5 minutes to »Platz der Einheit«; take tram 91 or 94 in the direction of »Bahnhof Pirschheide« (form. Hauptbahnhof), or tram 96 in the direction of »Schloss Charlottenhof« to »Luisenplatz«; walk from there about 5 minutes to »Grünes Gitter« park entrance.
– Take tram 91 to »Schloss Charlottenhof« then walk about 5 minutes to »Schloss Charlottenhof/Römische Bäder« park entrance.
• Arrival by car:
Follow the signs »Park Sanssouci« and use only the paying car parks »Luisenplatz«, »Am Schloss Sanssouci« or »Am Neuen Palais«. Illegally parked cars will be charged with tow-away fee.

New Garden
• Arrival at the station »Potsdam-Stadt« (national and local trains):
– Take tram 91, 93, 96 or 98 to »Platz der Einheit«, change to tram 95 in the direction of »Kapellenberg« to »Puschkinallee«; walk back about 50 metres and turn left in the Allee-Strasse; walk about 5 minutes to New Garden park entrance.
– Take tram 91, 93, 96 or 98 to »Platz der Einheit«, walk about 5 minutes to Bassinplatz, then take bus 695 in the direction of »Höhenstrasse« to »Schloss Cecilienhof«.
• Arrival at »Potsdam-Busbahnhof« (coach station) at Bassinplatz:
Take bus 695 in the direction of »Höhenstrasse« to »Schloss Cecilienhof«.
• Arrival by car:
Follow the signs »Neuer Garten/Cecilienhof« and use the paying car park »Am Schloss Cecilienhof« (no other parking facilities).

Babelsberg Park
• Arrival at the station »Drewitz« (local trains):
Take the trolley-bus in the direction of »Babelsberg-Nord« to »Sternwarte«; walk to the upper park entrance »Allee nach Glienicke«.
• Arrival at the station »Babelsberg« (local trains):
– Cross the street to the bus stop »Rathaus« and take the trolley as above.
– Take tram 94 in the direction of »Bahnhof Pirschheide« (form. Hauptbahnhof) to »Übergang Bruno-Baum-Strasse« and cross the overpass to the park.
• Arrival at Glienicker Brücke (Berlin bus 116/93 and Potsdam tram 3):
Walk about 15 minutes through Klein-Glienicke to Babelsberg Park entrance.
• Arrival by car:
– Follow the signs »Babelsberg-Nord« and »Klein-Glienicke«; parking is available at the »Park Brücke« entrance.
– Park in Klein-Glienicke and walk across the Park Bridge over the Teltow Canal to the park entrance. Parking is also available at the park entrance.

Hours

	Hours	Closed	Pause	Telephone
Sans Souci	Guided tours every 20 min. April–Sept.: 9:00 to 17.00 Feb., March and Oct.: 9:00 to 16:00 Nov.–Jan.: 9:00 to 15:00	1st and 3rd Mon. of every month	12:30 to 13:00	9 69 41 90
Ladies' Wing Damenflügel	9:00 to 17:00 (mid–May to mid–Oct. only)	Mondays Tuesdays	11:45 to 12:30	9 69 41 82
Sans Souci Picture Gallery Bildergalerie Sanssouci	Closed until 1995 (restoration)			
New Palace Neues Palais	Mid–Oct. to mid–May: guided tours only April–Sept.: 9:00 to 17:00 Feb., March and Oct.: 9:00 to 16:00 Nov.–Jan.: 9:00 to 15:00	2nd and 4th Mon. of every month	12:45 to 13:15	97 31 43
Theatre in New Palace Schloßtheater im Neuen Palais	According to programme (closed from Jan. to March) Tickets/Information: Potsdam/Information, Hans-Otto-Theater, Besucher-Service			97 31 43 2 11 00 2 80 06 93
Café in New Palace Schloßcafé im Neuen Palais	10:00 to 19:00	2nd Mon. of every month		97 28 69
New Chambers Neue Kammern	Guided tours every 20 min. April–Sept.: 9:00 to 17:00 Feb., March and Oct.: 9:00 to 16:00 Nov.–Jan.: 9:00 to 15:00·	Fridays	12:00 to 12:30	2 28 23
Orangery Palace (including Tower) Orangerieschloß mit Aussichtsturm	9:00 to 17:00 (mid–May to mid–Oct. only)	4th Thu. of every month	12:00 to 13:00	2 61 89

	Hours	Closed	Pause	Telephone
Chinese Tea House Chinesisches Teehaus	9:00 to 17:00 (mid-May to mid-Oct. only)	2nd Mon. of every month	12:00 to 12:45	97 36 28
Charlottenhof	9:00 to 17:00 (mid-May to mid-Oct. only)	4th Mon. of every month	12:30 to 13:00	97 27 74
Roman Baths Römische Bäder	9:00 to 17:00 (mid-May to mid-Oct. only)	3rd Mon. of every month	12:30 to 13:00	97 47 08
Pump House (mosque) Dampfmaschi-nenhaus (Moschee)	Mid-Oct. to mid-May. Sat. and Sun. only, 9:00 to 16:00 mid-May to mid-Oct.: Wed.-Sun., 9:00 to 17:00	Mondays and Tuesday	12:00 to 13:00	9 69 42 48
Hunting Lodge Stern Jagdschloß Stern	Saturdays and Sundays 10:00 to 17:00 (mid-May to mid-Oct. only)			62 12 44
Cecilienhof	Guided tours by appointment May–Oct.: 9:00 to 17:00 Nov.–April: 9:00 to 16:00	2nd and 4th Mon. of every month		9 69 42 44
Church of Peace in Sans Souci Park Friedens-kirche	Mid-May to mid-Oct.: 10:00 to 18:00 July and August: 2 organ concerts monthly May-Sept.: summer music, 1st Sat. of every month, 17:00			
Babelsberg Palace	April–Sept.: 9:00 to 17:00 Feb., March and Oct.: 9:00 to 16:00 Nov.–Jan.: 9:00 to 15:00	Mondays and Tuesdays	12:00 to 12:30	7 80 75

Visitor Service of the Sans Souci Palaces and Gardens Foundation
Am Grünen Gitter · Postfach 60 14 62 · 14414 Potsdam
Guide referrals for park and palace tours (group or individual):
telephone and fax 2 38 19 · 8:00 to 16:30

Sans Souci Information
Am Schloss Sanssouci · 14414 Potsdam
Opening hours: April–Sept. 9:00 to 17:00, Feb., March and Oct.: 9:00 to 16:00, Nov. and Dec.: 9:00 to 15:00 · Telephone: 2 20 51

Potsdam-Information · Tourist Office
Am Alten Markt · Friedrich-Ebert-Strasse 5 · 14467 Potsdam
Opening hours: 9:00 to 18:00 · Telephone: 2 11 00